TAIJIQUAN

CHEN TAIJI 38 FORM AND APPLICATIONS

TAIJIQUAN

CHEN TAIJI 38 FORM AND APPLICATIONS

REN GUANG YI

TUTTLE PUBLISHING
Boston · Rutland,Vermont · Tokyo

First published in 2003 by Tuttle Publishing, an imprint of Periplus Editions (HK) Ltd., with editorial offices at 153 Milk Street, Boston, Massachusetts 02109.

Library of Congress Cataloging-in-Publication Data
Yi, Ren Guang, 1965-
    Taijiquan : Chen taiji 38 form and applications / Ren Guang Yi—1st ed.
       p. cm.
    Incudes bibliographical references.
ISBN: 0-8048-3526-8 (pbk)
LCC No.: 2003054034

Distributed by

North America, Latin America, and Europe
Tuttle Publishing
Distribution Center
Airport Industrial Park
364 Innovation Drive
North Clarendon, VT 05759-9436
Tel: (802) 773-8930
Fax: (802) 773-6993
Email: info@tuttlepublishing.com

Asia Pacific
Berkeley Books Pte. Ltd.
130 Joo Seng Road
#06-01/03 Olivine Building
Singapore 368357
Tel: (65) 6280-3320
Fax: (65) 6280-6290
Email: inquiries@periplus.com.sg

Japan
Tuttle Publishing
Yaekari Bldg., 3F
5-4-12 Ōsaki, Shinagawa-ku
Tokyo 141-0032
Tel: (03) 5437-0171
Fax: (03) 5437-0755
Email: tuttle-sales@gol.com

First edition
08 07 06 05 04 03 9 8 7 6 5 4 3 2 1

Text design by Linda Carey
Printed in Canada

CONTENTS

FOREWORD

Few books have been written on Chen Style Taijiquan in English. Master Ren Guang Yi hopes this practical book will expose the technical richness of the original version of Taiji to both novice and advanced martial artists. Based on the teaching of Master Ren and the International Chen Style Taijiquan Association (ICSTA), this work was undertaken to make Chen Taiji more accessible to Taiji enthusiasts of all styles.

The book introduces Chen Taiji's history, concepts, and techniques in a succinct format for the layman. Using the 38 Movement Short Form as the exemplar, the book illustrates the modern canon of Chen Taiji, while revealing the historical underpinnings that comprise the foundation of Chen style practice. First, Chen Taiji's history is summarized, with a lineage chart revealing the main proponents of the Lao Jia and Xin Jia versions of the art. An explication of Eleventh-Generation Standard Bearer Grandmaster Chen Xiaowang's 38 Movement Short Form, as taught by his protégé, Master Ren, follows. The next section offers guidelines for general forms practice, along with advice on the proper execution of power-issuing. The concepts and training of Chen style self-defense follow with accompanying photos of select applications from the 38 Form. The last section discusses the practical application of basic Taiji theory for Taijiquan boxers of any style.

While most English writings on Chen Taiji identify the art's leading masters by their Chen family generation, Master Ren uses the actual Chen Taiji *martial art* lineage designations found in Chinese texts, to accurately designate the art's proponents generationally.

As long-term students of Master Ren, Stephan Berwick and Jose Figueroa assembled this book based on Master Ren's desire to produce a practical Chen Taiji guide in English. To that end, Mr. Berwick researched and wrote the sections on history, concepts, and training, while Mr. Figueroa wrote the detailed description of the form and applications, based on the direct teachings of Master Ren.

Master Ren, Mr. Berwick, and Mr. Figueroa would like to thank Douglas Fisher and David Goncalves for the photography and layout, Linda DiSantis for the supplementary photography, and Patricia Sadiq for the original lineage chart and cover design. Also, Master Ren's long-time student, Gregory Pinney, deserves thanks for the use of his academy, Hua Mountain Kung Fu, for the photographic setting.

Chen Taiji's Lao Jia and Xin Jia Lineage

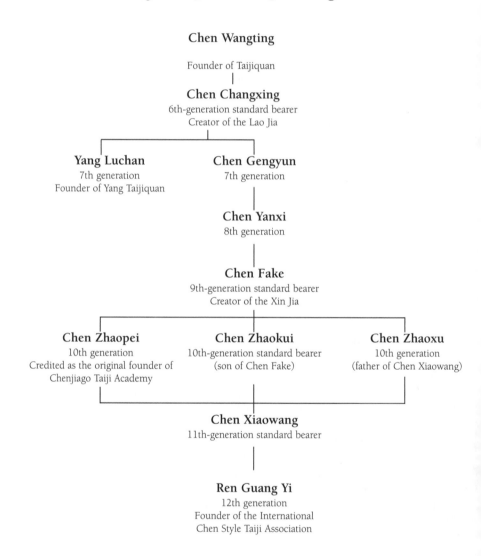

Chen Wangting

Founder of Taijiquan

Chen Changxing
6th-generation standard bearer
Creator of the Lao Jia

Yang Luchan
7th generation
Founder of Yang Taijiquan

Chen Gengyun
7th generation

Chen Yanxi
8th generation

Chen Fake
9th-generation standard bearer
Creator of the Xin Jia

Chen Zhaopei
10th generation
Credited as the original founder of
Chenjiago Taiji Academy

Chen Zhaokui
10th-generation standard bearer
(son of Chen Fake)

Chen Zhaoxu
10th generation
(father of Chen Xiaowang)

Chen Xiaowang
11th-generation standard bearer

Ren Guang Yi
12th generation
Founder of the International
Chen Style Taiji Association

CHEN TAIJIQUAN: HISTORY AND EVOLUTION

Chen boxing originated in an era of change. The late Ming dynasty (seventeenth century) was a time of enormous transition in China. As the Manchu-led Chings assumed power, forming China's last dynastic period, much of Ming society lost its place. As the emergence of Ching rule created societal upheaval firearms came into use. Military officers, scholars, and other important groups lost their status as the Ching leaders fell victim to the era of foreign domination that swept much of the non-Western world.

CHEN WANGTING
Chen family 9th generation
Founder of Taijiquan

Chen boxing's founder, the respected Ming general Chen Wangting, lived at the advent of this era. With his military status dwindling in importance, Chen Wangting found himself searching for a new martial expression later in his life. He described his retirement as focused on teaching and "creating movements of boxing."[1] His study resulted in his deriving a new martial art from earlier boxing concepts and techniques, to create a sophisticated, and for the time, modern interpretation of traditional Chinese martial art. These "movements" were taken from the battle-tested martial arts of North China and imbued with metaphysical concepts that flourished during the Ming dynasty. Thus a highly evolved martial art was born during one of China's most vivid periods of evolution.

Chen Wangting's boxing inspiration developed into an extremely sophisticated boxing style that, according to available history, was the first system of boxing to train fighters based on Jingluo and Daoyin—the ancient Chinese concepts of internal energy circulation. With a deep understanding of these related physiological concepts, Chen Wangting reinterpreted powerful Northern Chinese boxing techniques recorded in the famed general Qi Jiguang's seminal text *Canons of Boxing*. He refined these popular long-range boxing techniques based on Jingluo concepts and his theory of "hiding firmness with softness" to build a uniquely powerful, yet health-giving form of self-defense.

---

[1] Liuxin Gu, *Chen Style Taijiquan*, Hai Feng and Zhaohua 1984, p. 4.

This unprecedented achievement in Chinese boxing was first recorded in his *Song of the Canon of Boxing*.

Chen Wangting wrote, "Actions are so varied and executed in such a way as to be wholly unpredictable to the enemy and I rely on twining actions and a host of hand-touching movements."[2] "Hand-touching" refers to what came to be known as *tui shou* or "push hands"—the popular partner training used to develop sensitivity and neutralization skills. "Twining" refers to the unique coiling nature of Chen boxing techniques.

> [Chen style] contains spiral-like twining actions, alternatively extending and withdrawing, being tight and loose, and firm and soft. The boxer is required to direct the Qi (literally "breath," referring to inner vital energy) by mental exertion and to let the Qi, which should be concentrated, spread through the whole body. Qi is originated from the pubic region and pressed through the whole body by gradually twisting one's body with the waist as an axis. The Qi is pressed upward to the tips of the fingers by twisting the arms and wrists, and downward to the toes by twisting the knees and ankles. Having reached the extremities, the Qi then returns to the pubic region. Such practice results in strengthened offensive and defensive force of the body and limbs as well as increased explosiveness of such force. In this way, Chen Wangting not only assimilated but also developed the Jingluo theory.[3]

Also described as *chan szu jin* or "silk-reeling energy," the subtle coiling of the joints of Chen Taiji is the key to the legendary power displayed by Chen boxers.

> Coiling power is all over the body. Putting it most simply, there is coiling inward and coiling outward, which both appear once (one) moves. There is one (kind of coiling) when left hand is in front and right hand is behind; (or when) right hand is in front and left hand is behind; this one closes (the hands) with one conforming (movement). All of them should be moved naturally according to the (specific) postures.[4]

Like classical music or fine engineering, it was upon these proven concepts that Chen boxing and its later interpretations (such as Yang and Wu styles) came to be known as Taijiquan, the "Grand Ultimate Fist."

---

[2] Gu, p. 6.
[3] Gu, p. 5.
[4] Xin Chen (Internet)

10

38 Movement Short Form: Origin and Rationale

Form or routine training in Chen Taijiquan is crucial. It is the primary conditioning tool for the body and serves as the textbooks for Tai Ji's rich content. Rooted in time-tested boxing and power development, Tai Ji forms require years of repetitive practice and quality coaching for mastery. Thus it can be said, the practice of Chen style forms is akin to studying a well-written encyclopedia of boxing.

The original five-seven Chen family boxing forms were preserved and passed over five generations to Chen Chanxing (known as the teacher of Yang Luchan, founder of Yang Taijiquan). These original forms were distilled by Chen Chanxing into the "Old Frame," usually known as the "Old Style," or *Lao Jia*. Based on the original routines, the Lao Jia came to be composed of two core open-hand forms—*Yi Lu*, or the "Long" form (the foundation of all Tai Chi styles) and the *Er Lu*, popularly known as the vigorous *Pao Chui*, or "Cannon Fist." Chen Chanxing's creation of the Lao Jia remains intact to this day.

In 1928, the gifted ninth-generation grandmaster, Chen Fake, came to Beijing from Chenjiagou village to teach the Lao Jia. Perhaps Chen style's greatest master, Chen Fake remains legendary to this day. He taught and defeated many established fighters according to well-documented accounts. Existing photos of his performances reveal an uncommon skill of the highest order in his stances, flexibility, posture, precision, and spirit. As evidence of his genius, he refined the Lao Jia, reapplying his ancestor Chen Wangting's potent concepts of twining power, to form the *Xin Jia*, or "New Frame," versions of both the Yi Lu and Er Lu. Chen Fake imbued the forms with a more obvious use of twining and coiling movement interpreted through *chin-na* (joint-locking) techniques. He lengthened the forms, adding more techniques per section to better express highly developed *fa-jing*—the issuing of explosive, flexible power. Chen Fake's creation and execution of Xin Jia embodied Chen Wangting's pioneering concept of twining power to levels probably not seen in generations before his time. As a result, his interpretation of the classic empty-hand routines caused Chen Taiji to evolve to a higher standard.

In today's China, competition Chen Taiji forms are largely derived from Xin Jia. However, the forms often exhibit an exaggerated use of coiling that does not reflect the subtlety inherent in Chen Fake's refinement. It can be argued that without a base of classical Lao Jia—as Chen Fake had—the practice of Xin Jia may exhibit serious flaws.

Noting this, the present-day eleventh-generation Chen Taiji standard bearer, Grandmaster Chen Xiaowang, created the 38 Movement Short Form as the foundation form for modern Chen practitioners. The 38 techniques that constitute the routine combine select techniques of Xin Jia with the classic movement of Lao Jia. This rich balance distinguishes the techniques that compose the 38 Form as assimilable samples of Chen boxing's comprehensive body of techniques.

Grandmaster Chen's choice of 38 fundamental Chen techniques captures the essence of Lao Jia and Xin Jia. The 38 Form distills Chen Taijiquan to core fundamentals, building a well-rounded foundation for the novice. Normally 4–5 minutes in duration, the form is half the length of the Lao Jia long form (Yi Lu) and does not have the repetitive movement normally found in traditional Chinese boxing forms. Heralded as a rare achievement for the teaching and practice of Chen Taijiquan, the 38 Form builds foundation skills in both Xin Jia and Lao Jia. As such, the 38 Form grounds the student in the diversity of Chen technique from the very start.

Getting Started: Practicing the 38 Movement Short Form

The 38 Form is divided into four sections that contain classic Chen techniques including joint locking, punching, jabbing, leaping, and kicking. To master such a plethora of techniques, the following guidelines should be adhered to when practicing the 38 Form and all Chen Taiji forms.

- Focus on the precision of single techniques.
- During and after memorization, execute the combinations slowly.
- The back must remain straight with relaxed shoulders.
- Keep the limbs bent and the groin open.
- When stepping forward or to the side, the heel of the stepping foot touches first.
- Clearly distinguish which leg is weight-bearing, or "full," and which is "empty."
- Move with an obvious balance of force, directed from the Dantian.

Of note, practice of the 38 Form introduces fa jing (explosive relaxed power) to the novice. Executing quick strikes, throws, and locks with relaxed power is common in Chinese martial arts, but highly developed in Chen Taiji's expression of fa jing. Most punches, kicks, palm strikes, and throwing movements are normally practiced with fa jing in the 38 Form. As a hallmark of the style, the practitioner should aspire to Chen Taiji's unique expression of fa jing. In so doing, note the following:

- After about three months of practice, execute the strikes with light fa jing.
- Strikes with fa jing should be relaxed, speedy, and firmly focused at contact.
- Exhale with a natural force when striking with fa jing.
- Control the direction of energy with a clear mental focus or intention known as "yi."
- The body should be relaxed up to and just after the point of impact.
- The waist should torque with looseness and speed.
- When issuing power strikes, adhere to the rules of *chan szu jin.*

The Chen Style Taijiquan 38 Movement Short Form

Section 1

1: Preparing Form

2: Buddha's Warrior Attendant Pounds Mortar

3: White Crane Spreads Its Wings

4: Moving Three Steps Forward

5: Walk Obliquely

6: Brush the Knee

7: Kick Forward and Twist Step

8: Hidden Hand Fist

9: Turn the Waist and Circle the Fist

10: Double-Hand Push

Section 2

11: Change Palms Three Times

12: Fist under Elbow

13: Step Back and Swirl the Arms

14: Step Back and Press Elbow

15: White Snake Darts Its Tongue

16: Flash the Back

17: Kick Forward and Twist Step

18: Blue Dragon Pops Out of the Water

19: Punch Hits the Ground

Section 3

20: Double-Jump Kicks

21: Fist Protecting Heart

22: Frontal Block

23: Rear Block

24: Kick with Right Heel

25: Kick with Left Heel

26: Fair Lady Works at Shuttle

Section 4

27: Lazily Tying Coat

28: Six Sealings, Four Closings

29: Single Whip

30: Dragon Sparrow on Ground

31: Step Forward Salute the Seven Stars

32: Small Catch and Hitting

33: Wave Hands Like Clouds

34: High Pat on Horse

35: Wave Hands and Sweep Lotus with One Leg

36: Overhead Cannon

37: Buddha's Warrior Attendant Pounds Mortar

38: Closing Form

THE PALM

The palm is a general hand position used in Chen Taiji boxing.

It serves as a vessel that transmits *qi* (energy).

When executing this hand position, relax the fingers and open the center of the palm.

The general application of this hand position is striking and grabbing.

THE FIST

The fist position in Chen Taiji boxing uses all sides of the fist for striking with the extreme force of concentrated qi.

Before striking, relax the fist. At the moment of impact, the fist completely tightens, then immediately relaxes.

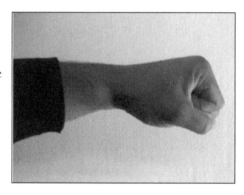

THE HOOK

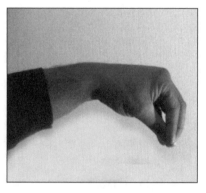

To form the hook hand position, press the four fingers against the thumb gently.

This should be done with the wrist slightly bent and relaxed.

Use this hand position for releases of *qin-na* (joint locks).

The top part of the wrist joint is a part of the hand usually used when striking.

Chen Taiji Stance *Left* Side

The weight is on the *left* side of the body (70% on the left, 30% on the right).

Chen Taiji Stance *Right* Side

The weight is on the *right* side of the body (70% on the right, 30% on the left).

Chen Taiji Stance *Right* Back

The weight is on the *right* side of the body (70% on the left, 30% on the right).

Chen Taiji Stance *Left* Front

The weight is on the *left* side of the body (70% on the left, 30% on the right).

The Chen Style Taijiquan 38 Short Form Movement (Sanshiba)

Section 1

1: Preparing Form

2: Buddha's Warrior Attendant Pounds Mortar

3: White Crane Spreads Its Wings

4: Moving Three Steps Forward

5. Walk Obliquely

6: Brush the Knee

7: Kick Forward and Twist Step

8: Hidden Hand Fist

9: Turn the Waist and Circle the Fist

10: Double-Hand Push

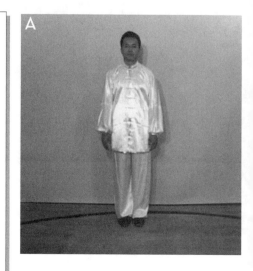

1: Preparing Form

A. Stand with the feet together.

B. Transfer your weight to the right leg and raise the left heel, bending the knee.

C. Step out to your left, placing the feet a shoulders' width apart. Lower your hips and rise slightly, but keep the knees bent.

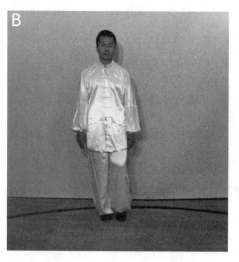 

2: Buddha's Warrior Attendant Pounds Mortar

A. Slowly raise both arms up to chest level.

B. Lower both arms directly toward the hips.

C. When the palms pass your navel, transfer your weight to the right as you bring both arms up to the left side of the body.

D. Transfer the weight to your left leg while turning your torso to the right.

E. Transfer the weight to the right foot and bring the left foot alongside the right leg.

F. Extend the left leg diagonally while keeping your weight on the right leg.

G. Circle both arms back and sweep them forward. Extend the left hand at shoulder level; circle the right palm by the right thigh as you bring the ball of the right foot parallel to the left (shoulders' width apart). Raise the right palm to chest height, palm up, as the left hand rests on top of it.

H. Gently turn the left palm over so that it is parallel to the right wrist.

I. As the left palm turns over, the right hand turns into a fist.

J. Lift the right knee up to waist level, while the right fist comes up parallel to the right shoulder.
Note: Place the left hand in front of the navel, with the palm facing up.

K. Bring the right foot down to a shoulders'-width-apart stance, dropping the right fist inside the left palm.

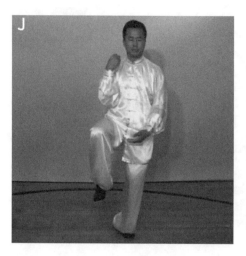 

3: WHITE CRANE SPREADS ITS WINGS

A. Transfer your weight to the right as you raise the right palm in a semicircle.

B. As you shift your weight to the left, circle the left hand up and lower the right hand to waist height.

C. With your weight on the left leg, extend the right heel in a right oblique position, and bring the left hand over so that it ends up on top of the right forearm.

D. Pivot the right foot to the left.
Note: The entire trunk of the body should turn while pivoting.

E. With your weight on the left leg, transfer your weight to the right and bring the right hand up to the right side of the body. The left hand should be parallel to the left knee, with fingers facing inward.

4: Moving Three Steps Forward

A. Circle the right hand down to your right thigh, while extending the left palm forward and extending the left heel diagonally.
Note: The weight should be on the right leg.

B. Circle the left palm downward, then transfer the weight to the left leg. Circle the right palm forward and extend the right heel diagonally.

C. Circle the right hand down so that it ends up by your right thigh; extend the left palm forward and extend the left heel diagonally.
Note: The weight should be on the right leg, and the stance is slightly wider than in the first two steps.

REVERSE ANGLE

5: WALK OBLIQUELY

A. While the left palm is extended, bend the elbow. As it crosses the body, turn your torso to the right.

B. Circle the right hand back so that it ends up by your right ear.

C. Transfer the weight to the left leg as you turn the torso to the left diagonal position.
Note: As the elbow passes the knee, the left palm changes into a hook position.

D. Extend the left hook at the left diagonal position, then glide the right palm (now by your left elbow) across toward the right as you turn your torso to the right.

E. Center your hips and arms, and allow the body to descend into a relaxed position.
Note: The weight should be mostly on the left leg, and both knees are bent.

6: Brush the Knee

A. Raise both arms over your head so that the backs of your wrists almost touch.

B. Whip both arms down so that they end up over the left knee.
   Note: Both palms are facing up, and the left arm is extended slightly more than the right.

C. Transfer the weight to the right leg, and fold the left arm over the right.

D. Raise the left knee while extending both arms forward and over the knee.
   Note: The left arm is slightly more extended than the right, and both palms are facing down and draped over the left knee.

7: Kick Forward and Twist Step

A. Pull back both palms so that they circle past the waist.

B. Extend the arms back to shoulder height, with the right wrist placed behind the left.

C. Step forward with the left foot.

D. Pivot half a turn. Turn the waist to the left as you transfer the weight to the left foot.

E. Step to the right with the right foot.

F. Slowly transfer the weight to the right leg.
Note: As this happens, separate the palms, ending with them wider than shoulders' width apart.

8: HIDDEN HAND FIST

A. Shift your weight to the left as you turn your body to the right. Pull your right fist back by your waist as you extend the left arm forward, palm up.

B. Transfer the weight to the right leg, as you lift the left leg.

C. Extend the left foot to the side.

D. Transfer the weight to the left foot, as you retract the left palm to the waist, and punch with the right fist on a diagonal.
Note: Although this is a fa jing movement, do it slowly until you develop the explosive power.

9: Turn the Waist and Circle the Fist

A. Keep your weight on the left leg. Turn your torso to the right as you bring your right fist over by your right knee, and your left fist up to chest height.

B. Shift your weight to the right leg as you circle your right fist.

C. Continue to circle your right arm counterclockwise.

D. Shift your weight to the left as you extend the right arm forward, fist facing up.

E. Retract your right fist to the right side of your head, and transfer your weight to the right leg. As this happens, place the left fist on the left hip.
Note: The left elbow should be parallel to the left knee.

10: DOUBLE-HAND PUSH

A. Extend both palms out to the right side of the body.

B. Sweep both palms across to the left as you transfer your weight to the left leg.

C. Turn your waist toward the left as you step forward, and extend both palms in front of your torso.

D. Transfer your weight to your right leg. Extend both palms forward.
   Note: Place the ball of your left foot slightly ahead of your right.

11: CHANGE PALMS THREE TIMES

A. Stand with your feet a shoulders' width apart. Extend the left palm out, keeping your weight on the right leg.

B. Extend your right palm forward as you turn your waist to the left and retract the left hand.

C. Extend the left palm out as you turn your waist to the right.
   Note: Your weight is on the right leg.

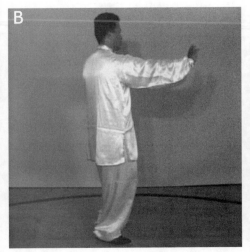

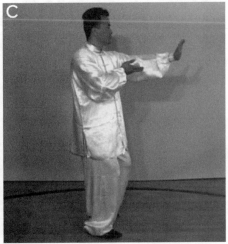

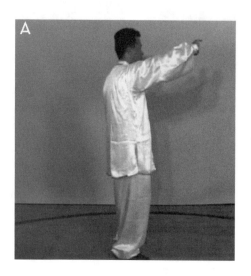

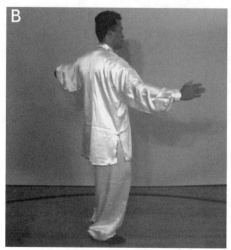

12: Fist under Elbow

A.–B. Circle the right hand forward as you circle the left hand down and back behind the left hip.

C.   Complete the circle with the left arm so that it ends up vertical, with the fingers facing up and the arm bent at the elbow 90 degrees.

D.   The right hand forms a fist directly beneath the left elbow.

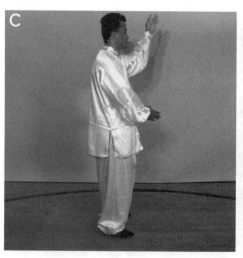

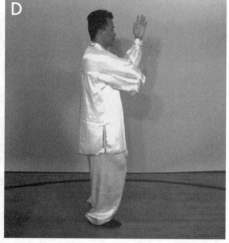

13: Step Back and Swirl the Arms

A. Bring your left hand down to the side of your body as you extend your right hand. While doing this, move your left foot backward diagonally, and extend your left hand back together with the left leg.

B. Circle your left hand so that it ends up by your left ear.

C. Extend your left hand forward and move your right foot and hand backwards.

D. Circle your right hand so that it ends up by your right ear.

E. Extend your right hand forward and move your left foot and hand backwards.

F. Bring the left hand forward to join with the right.

G. Transfer your weight to the left and move both hands to the left side of your body.

H. Transfer your weight back to the right.

I. Turn your torso to the right and lower the right hand.

J. Reach forward with the left hand and shift your weight to the left. Shift your weight back to the right and extend your right hand forward just past the right knee.

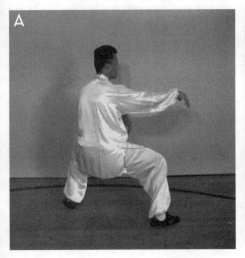

14: Step Back and Press Elbow

A.–B. Keep your weight on the left leg. Bring your right foot toward the left foot until they are a shoulders' width apart. Raise the left arm to the center of your chest, palm down.

B. Place the right palm down on the left elbow.
Note: The palms should be horizontal, and the blade of the hand extended.

C. Move the right elbow and the right leg backwards, keeping your weight on the left leg. Extend the left palm, facing out.

15: White Snake Darts Its Tongue

A. As you lean to the left, circle the left hand down (clockwise), and circle the right hand up (also clockwise).

B. Shift your weight to the right leg, circle the right palm down and to the right, while the left palm circles up and to the left.

C. Retract the right palm with the palm facing out, so that it ends up by your waist. The left palm is at shoulder height, facing up.

D. Transfer your weight to the left leg as you begin to bring the right hand forward.

E. Extend your right hand, with the palm facing up, past your waist.

F. Extend the right hand up (head height), while the left hand circles to the left thigh.

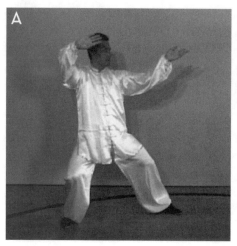

16: Flash the Back

A. Shift your weight to the right leg as you raise both palms to shoulder height.

B. Turn your left foot to the right, then transfer your weight onto it.

C.–E. Make a half-turn clockwise, swinging the right palm all the way around so that it ends up by your right knee.
Note: While doing this, your left palm will end up in front of your left shoulder, and the left elbow will be bent. Allow both hands to cross, then swing them down and circle them around.

17: Kick Forward and Twist Step

A.–C. Pull back both palms so that they circle past the waist. Continue circling your hands so they end up in front, at chest height. Extend the left foot and pivot a quarter-turn to the left.

D. Place the left foot down as you turn the waist to the left, and transfer the weight to the left foot.

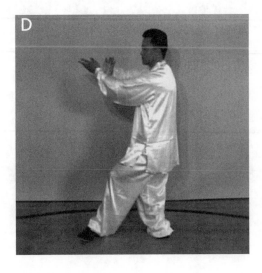

E. Transfer all weight to the left foot as you turn your body to the right.

F. Extend the right foot to the side, while keeping your weight on the left.

G. Transfer the weight to the right leg as your torso slowly turns to the left.

H. Extend both arms out to the side of the body.

I. Slowly sink both hips as you continue placing your weight on the right leg. *Note:* Maintain approximately 70 percent of your weight on the right leg and 30 percent on the left. Arms and legs should match in width.

18: Blue Dragon Pops Out of the Water

A. Transfer your weight to the right leg as you sink both hands toward your waist.

B. Extend the right palm to the left knee as you place the left hand by the right forearm in a fist.
Note: The left hand is placed near the right forearm with the fist facing up.

C. Extend the left fist to the left knee as you retract the right palm to the right hip.
Note: While doing this, transfer your weight to the left.

19: Punch Hits the Ground

A. Extend both hands diagonally to the left.

B. Slowly pivot the right foot as you turn your body to the right.

C. Transfer your weight to the right leg as you bring the left foot up.

D. Step out on a diagonal with the left foot while maintaining the hands on the right side of the body. The weight is on the right leg.

E. Circle the left hand across the body as you circle back and around.

F. Transfer your weight to the left foot as you circle the left fist across the left knee.

G. As you transfer your weight from the right to the left leg, punch down with the right hand as you extend the left arm to the left.

20: DOUBLE-JUMP KICKS

A.–B. Circle the left fist over the right forearm (clockwise), as you circle the right fist downward.

C. Transfer your weight to the right leg as you circle the right arm back and the left arm down.

D. Pivot the left foot to the right.

E. Transfer your weight to your left foot as you turn your waist to the right.

F. Circle the left arm forward and up past the left ear as you circle the right arm down.

G. Transfer your weight to the right leg as you lift the left leg waist-high. The left arm circles down as the right arm circles up.

H. Push off the right leg as you swing the right leg up past your waist, using the right palm to smack the right instep. The left hand circles back and around.

I. Land on the left foot. The left hand is behind, and the right hand is in front.
Note: When landing, slightly bend the left knee to absorb the impact of the landing.

21: Fist Protecting Heart

A. Step toward the right, swinging both palms in the same direction.

B. Transfer all your weight to the right foot as you bring the left foot parallel to the right.

C. Circle the arms to the right as you step out to the left.

D. Transfer the weight to the left side of your body as you swing your arms in the same direction.

E. Pull back the right foot so that it's parallel to the left.

F. Begin to lower the left side of your body as both hands turn to fists.

G. Step out to the right and turn your waist to the left.

H. Turn your waist to the right.

I. Place the right fist over the right knee, as the left turns to the front of the chest. *Note*: The weight is on the left.

J. Transfer your weight to the right as you circle the right arm counterclockwise.

K.–L. Place the right fist directly over the left one as you sink your weight on the right leg. *Note*: Put your weight on the right leg and extend the left foot on a diagonal.

22: FRONTAL BLOCK

A. Push with both hands to the left as you transfer your weight in the same direction.

B. Transfer your weight back to the right leg as you circle the left hand counterclockwise past the left knee.

C. Step forward with the left leg diagonally, while continuing to circle the left hand counterclockwise.
Note: Your weight is on your right leg.

D.–E. Transfer your weight to the left leg as you circle the left hand upward.

F. Bring the right leg forward so that it ends up parallel to the left leg.

23: Rear Block

A. Transfer your weight to the left foot as you circle the right hand toward the right leg.

B. Transfer your weight to the right side of your body as you circle the right hand clockwise.

C. Circle the left palm down toward the left thigh as you transfer your weight to the right.

D. Transfer your weight to the left as the right hand circles down to the right (clockwise).

E. Step out to the right.

F. Sink your weight on the left leg as you step out to the right.
Note: Weight distribution is approximately 70 percent on the left leg and 30 percent on the right.

24: KICK WITH RIGHT HEEL

A. Circle the right hand clockwise and transfer your weight to the right.

B. Circle the right hand until it extends to the far right.

C. Transfer your weight to the left as the right hand circles under the left.

D. Raise the right knee to waist height as you turn the hands over the right knee.

E.–F. Extend your arms to the side as you kick out with the right leg.

25: KICK WITH LEFT HEEL

A. Place the right heel to the side of your body.

B. Pivot to the right as you turn your torso in the same direction.

C. Transfer your weight to the right leg as you continue turning right.

D. Step out to the left while circling the left hand so that it ends up over the left knee.

E. Circle the left hand past the waist (counterclockwise).

F. Continue circling the left hand as you transfer your weight to the left leg.

G. Extend the left hand as you transfer your weight to the left.

H.–I. Transfer your weight to the right as you circle both hands together. Lift the left knee, bringing the left foot close to the right knee.

J. Fold your hands over as you prepare to kick with the left foot.

K. Kick out with the left foot as you extend the hands (at chest height) to the sides of the body.

26: Fair Lady Works at Shuttle

A.   Place the left foot down in front of you.

B.   Transfer your weight to the left leg as you circle the right arm forward.

C.   Extend the right arm forward as you step forward with the right foot.

D.–F. Continue circling both arms (clockwise) past the waist. Continue to circle until the arms end up in front again.

G. With your weight on the left leg, begin to lift your arms up.

H. Bring the right knee up to waist height.

I. Step out with the right leg.

J.–K. Leap and thrust the left palm forward while making a half-turn in mid air. Thrust the left palm forward and complete a half-turn.

L. After turning, your right palm is up, and the left palm is by your left thigh.

SECTION 4

COMMENT

Section 4 completes the photo section of the 38 Form. It builds upon the foundation established in the first three sections, so you should try to refine these earlier sections before learning the final section of the form.

To achieve the full benefits of Taiji, Chen-style training expects you to perform multiple forms in each training session. When you have a solid understanding of the structure and correct presentation of the entire form, you can continue with the "Applications" section beginning on page 72. It introduces the use of Chen Taiji in fighting applications.

27: Lazily Tying Coat

A. Transfer your weight to the left as you lower the right arm and raise the left.

B. Circle the left arm (clockwise) to the right side of the body, as the right palm circles in the same direction. The left palm ends up on top of the right forearm.

C. Turn the waist slightly to the left as you transfer your weight to the right leg.

D. The weight slowly transfers to the right as you circle the right hand in the same direction.

E. Extend the right palm out as the left hand glides across the midsection and is placed directly beneath the navel.
   Note: The left palm faces up.

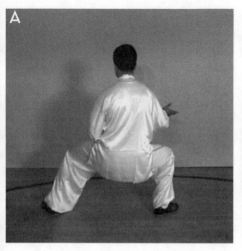

28: Six Sealings, Four Closings

A.–B. Circle both arms clockwise down toward the waist.

C. Circle the arms upward, clockwise, as you place the left wrist behind the right forearm.

D. Continue to circle to the right as you extend both arms out, then circle up.

E. Transfer your weight to the left as you turn your waist in the same direction.

F.   Extend both arms wide.

G.   While the waist turns to the left, circle both palms past both ears.

H.–I. Gently begin to extend both arms to the right side of the body.

J.   Shift your body weight to the right leg as you extend both arms to the right side. *Note*: Both palms should be facing down.

29: SINGLE WHIP

A.–B. Gently circle the right palm behind your body, then form a hook. As you do this, gently extend the left palm across the left side of the body, with the palm facing up.

C. Extend the right hook to the right diagonal position as you retract the left palm to the center of the waist.

D.–E. Extend the left foot to the left and gently place the heel down, then smoothly transfer your weight from the right to the left. Glide the left palm horizontally to the left side of the body.

F. Gently lower your weight to the left and sink in both hips, while the left palm settles with fingers facing upward.

 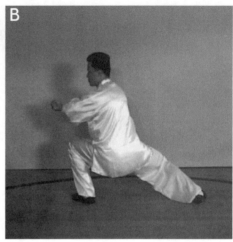

30: Dragon Sparrow on Ground

A. Transfer your weight to the left leg as both hands turn into fists.

B. Circle the right fist (clockwise) so that it ends up under the left fist.
   Note: Both fists are over the left knee.

C. Transfer your weight to the right leg as you circle both right and left hands clockwise.

D. Shift your weight to the right leg while extending both hands, and lower your weight onto the right hip.

31: Step Forward Salute the Seven Stars

A. Transfer your weight to the left foot as you bring the left fist up and the right fist down.

B. Circle the right fist under the left fist, and step forward on a diagonal with the right foot.

C. Transfer your weight to the right foot.

32: SMALL CATCH AND HITTING

A. Sink your weight on the right leg as you open both fists to an open-hand position.

B. Maintain all your weight on the right leg as you bring the left knee to waist height.

C. Step out on a diagonal with your left leg, while extending both hands, as shown above.

D. Raise the left hand up as you transfer your weight to the left leg.

E. While keeping your weight on the left leg, sway both hands to the left.

F. Change the direction of the hands as you transfer your weight to the right leg.

G. Lower your weight on the right leg as you drop the right palm so that the fingers are pointing up.
Note: Figure **G2** is the reverse image of the posture.

H. Transfer your weight to the left foot as you extend the right palm out. The left arm is horizontal and bent at the elbow.

33: Wave Hands Like Clouds

A.–B. Move the left hand down and circle it counterclockwise, while you move the right hand up and circle it clockwise.

C. Continue to circle both palms as you move the left hand up and the right hand down, while transferring your weight to the left.

D.–E. Continue circling both hands as you reverse their up/down positions. While doing this, transfer your weight to the left leg.

F. When the weight is completely on the left leg, step with the right foot behind the left foot as you circle your arms.

G. Transfer your weight to the right leg as you turn your waist to the left.

H.–I. Step out with the left foot as you circle the left hand down and the right hand up.

J. Transfer your weight to the left foot as you circle the left arm counterclockwise and the right hand clockwise.

K. Step with the right leg behind the left foot as you continue to circle the arms.

L. Keep your weight on the right foot, and step out to the left.
Note: Circle the arms in opposite directions as you step out; the left hand moves counterclockwise, and the right hand moves clockwise.

34: HIGH PAT ON HORSE

A. Keep your weight on the right side, and step to the left while extending the left palm to the left.

B.–C. Turn to the left and transfer your weight to the left foot. Place the left palm over the right wrist. Step out to the right with the right foot.

D. Turn your waist to the left as you rotate the arms so that the palms are facing down.

E.–F. Extend both palms outward, as you transfer your weight to the right leg.

G. Transfer your weight to the left as you circle the right hand back and the left hand across to the right. Pivot the right foot in toward your torso.

H.–I. Turn your waist to the left as you press the right elbow to the left palm. As you do this, circle the left foot back (counterclockwise) so it ends up parallel to the right foot.

J.–K. Maintain the weight on the right leg, extend the right hand, and bring the left hand to the center of the waist.
Note: The left palm is facing up.

35: Wave Hands and Sweep Lotus with One Leg

A.   Transfer your weight to the right foot as both arms circle (clockwise).

B.   Turn your waist to the right as you circle the hands (clockwise). Transfer your weight to the left leg.

C.   Pivot the right foot to the right, as the left palm is placed over the right forearm.

D.   Transfer your weight to the right as you circle both hands to the right.

E.–F. Step out on a diagonal with the left foot, while extending both palms.

G. Transfer your weight to the left foot as you circle both hands (clockwise).

H. Continue circling the arms in the same direction, as you bring the right foot forward.

I. Raise the right foot off the ground as you circle the right leg (clockwise).

J. As you raise the right foot, let both hands descend toward the right foot.

K. Slap the right instep with the left palm, and the right palm to the right heel.

36: Overhead Cannon

A.   Extend the right foot down as you circle both arms backwards.

B.–C. Circle both fists over your head, on the right side of the body, as you step back with the right foot.

D.–E. Pull back both fists toward the torso, as you turn your waist to the right. Transfer your weight to the right leg.

F.   Transfer your weight forward to the left leg as you punch with both fists at chest height.

37: Buddha's Warrior Attendant Pounds Mortar

A.–C. Open both hands as you circle both arms back. As you do this, transfer your weight to your right leg.

D. Transfer the weight forward to the left leg as you circle both hands back and past the waist.

E.–F. Extend the left hand forward with the right hand following, while bringing the right leg forward so that it ends up parallel to the left leg.

G. Bring the right foot parallel to the left, and bring the left palm on top of the right forearm. Gently turn the left palm over so that it is parallel to the right wrist. *Note:* As you turn the left palm over, the right hand turns into a fist.

H. Lift the right fist to the right shoulder, as you lift the right knee up to waist height. *Note:* Place the left hand in front of the navel, with the palm facing up.

I. Allow the right foot to come down at a shoulders'-width-apart stance while the right fist ends up inside the left palm.

38: Closing Form

A.–C. Extend both hands out and circle them down past the sides of your body.

D. Slowly straighten both knees.

E. Transfer your weight to the right leg.

F. Bring your left foot parallel to the right foot, and slowly stand erect.

Chen Taijiquan for Combat:
Applications of the 38 Movement Short Form

Mastery of Chen Taijiquan free-fighting begins with an understanding of the style's distinct usage. The secrets of Chen Taiji applications become more apparent with forms practice. This "shadow boxing" builds the practitioner's vocabulary of the fighting techniques recorded in the routines.

When a student's technical knowledge is internalized with forms training, the student can commence applications practice. The deadly hand, foot, knee, and elbow strikes are practiced in pairs, and often with full contact. Techniques from the forms are isolated and performed at varying speeds to build responsiveness and internalize Chen Taiji's unique approach to combat. The techniques are then integrated in "push hands" or *tui shou* practice and then in sparring and free-fighting. Such training leads to the goals of Chen style combat.

Six Sealings, Four Closings

Concerted application practice usually begins when the student approaches the intermediate level. Chen practitioners commence free-fighting practice from the base of push hands, which induces a fluid use of chin-na, neutralizing throws, and shoulder strikes. This stage is the most important for Taiji combat training. Considered the third of five stages of combat development in Chen Taijiquan, application training fortifies tui shou practice. One's basic push hands skill is utilized in the practice of applications. At this stage, hand, foot, knee, and elbow strikes are practiced repetitively with a partner. Techniques are isolated and performed at various speeds to build responsiveness and internalize the style's combat usage. The following training approaches are recommended for the novice combat trainee. With proper coaching this type of practice seems gradual, but actually teaches plenty of technique in a short time.

- With a partner, gradually practice the applications in a rehearsed format.
- Students should emphasize heavy repetition of single techniques first, and then progress to form-derived combinations.
- When trainees are able to perform a variety of applications competently at high speed, technique practice should not be overrehearsed.
- The goal of this stage is to build a vocabulary of technique that will form the basis of a student's arsenal.

As a complete fighting art, Chen Taiji consists of a wide variety of techniques applied with all the extremities. The following applications are culled from the 38 Movement Short Form as taught by Master Ren. The techniques were chosen as classic introductions to Chen boxing applications for the novice and to help the advanced student further his or her understanding of Chen Taiji's usage. Master Ren's execution of the 38 Movement Short Form and its applications reveals the practicality and precision characteristic of the professional Taiji boxer.

The following applications were chosen directly from the 38 Form to illustrate classical Chen Taiji's practical usage in combat.

HIDDEN HAND FIST

WALK OBLIQUELY

FLASH THE BACK

BUDDHA'S WARRIOR ATTENDANT POUNDS MORTAR

SINGLE WHIP A

SIX SEALINGS, FOUR CLOSINGS

SINGLE WHIP B

OVERHEAD CANNON

BRUSH THE KNEE

HIDDEN HAND FIST

A. When you are attacked from the front and rear, first use your peripheral vision to determine the space between you and the attackers.

B. When you are touched, move the left foot forward while the left hand blocks across your body. As this happens, press the right elbow backward so that the attacker cannot complete the rear choke hold.

C. Strike behind you with the left elbow, as you punch forward with the right.
Note: This should happen simultaneously.

D. Follow through by turning your torso to the left.
Note: The weight is transferred to the left foot as you punch.

WALK OBLIQUELY

A. When confronted by an opponent, prepare your stance by lowering the hips and bending the knees.

B. As the opponent punches, step in with the left foot and trap his right wrist with your right hand. Place your left hand at the attacker's left elbow.

C. Turn your waist to the right vigorously, transferring your weight to the right leg.

D. While executing the throw, be sure to follow through with the left palm. *Note:* Apply pressure on the attacker's right shoulder.

FLASH THE BACK

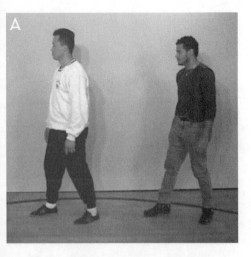

A. With your back to the attacker, begin to sink in the hips and knees.

B. When you feel the hand placed on your right shoulder, transfer your weight to the left leg as you turn your body to the right.

C. Turn to the right as you transfer your weight to the left foot. The right elbow circles clockwise over the attacker's wrist.

D. Continue turning to the right, and extend your right hand to grab the attacker's arm.

E. Slide your right hand down the attacker's arm and grab the attacker's wrist.

F. Turn your torso to the right as you pull the attacker's body down, exposing the neck. Then use the heel of the left hand to deliver a strong blow to the attacker's neck.

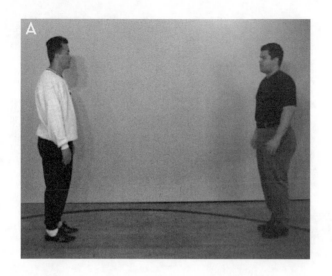

BUDDHA'S WARRIOR ATTENDANT POUNDS MORTAR

A. Stand facing your opponent and prepare by sinking the hips and knees.

B. Step forward to defend against a kick, and deflect its force to the left.

C. Circle the left hand (counterclockwise) to block the attacker's punch.

D. Slide the left hand to the attacker's wrist as you transfer your weight to the left leg. The right palm follows the transfer of weight.

E. Strike the center of the attacker's body with the right palm.

F. Pull with your left hand on the attacker's right wrist, and push with the right palm into the attacker's torso.

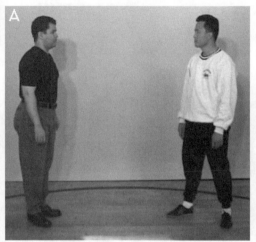 

SINGLE WHIP A

A.–B. While you are standing, an attacker reaches for your right wrist. Move your hand in the direction of the grab without resistance.

C. Turn your right wrist toward your torso while turning to the left, then grab the attacker's wrist with the left hand.

D. After switching hands, continue turning to the left while sliding out the right elbow.

E. Extend the right wrist to the attacker's jaw. The point of impact is the back of the hand. Pull the attacker's left arm in the opposite direction, and turn your entire torso to the left simultaneously.

Note: Use the waist for the power of the strike to the jaw.

Six Sealings, Four Closings

A.–B. Trap the attacker's right arm and pull it clockwise to control the wrist and elbow.

C.–D. Slide the attacker's left arm under the right arm as you turn to the left. Step forward and drop into a wide and low stance, with the right knee between the attacker's legs.

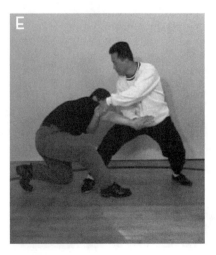

E. Lift up the attacker's left arm as you press down on his right arm.

F. Release both arms and slide your hands immediately to the attacker's shoulder.

G. Turn your waist to the right, shift your weight to the right leg, and thrust the palms down.

SINGLE WHIP B

A.–B. While the attacker traps your right arm, rotate the right elbow counterclockwise. Bring the attacker's right arm closer to your chest, trapping it with your left hand. Peel your right hand free from the attacker's grasp.

C. Extend your right arm, striking the attacker's jaw with the wrist. Use your left hand to turn the attacker's right wrist counterclockwise.

D. Turn your waist to the left as you continue to extend your right arm.
Note: Continue to control the attacker's right wrist.

OVERHEAD CANNON

A.–B. Circle your right hand clockwise to intercept the attacker's right hand, then press down with your left hand onto the attacker's right elbow.

C.–D. Pull the attacker's body forward as you lift your right leg and place it directly behind the attacker's right leg. Strike the attacker's neck with the right hand, and push back with your right leg.

E. Turn your entire body to the left while throwing the attacker to the floor.

BRUSH THE KNEE

A.–B. Use your arms to deflect the attacker's hands and open his arms. Next, quickly slide both arms past his arms and trap his head with both hands.

C. Pull the attacker's head down as you bring your left knee up, striking the head or chin.

Note: Both the knee and the arms come together simultaneously.

A FINAL NOTE ON FIGHTING APPLICATIONS

There are multiple ways to execute the fighting applications shown here, depending on the situation. To make any real progress in this area, you should seek guidance from a qualified and experienced teacher.

Balance of Forces:
Yin and Yang in Chen Taijiquan

For both combat and health, Chen Taiji requires that the body achieve a state of physical and mental balance based on the distinction between the opposing forces of Yin and Yang. These forces can be defined as hard and soft, fast and slow, heavy and light, erect and angled—or, as defined by Chen Xiaowang, empty and full. Chen style exhibits a pervasive balance of these sometimes opposing forces. It is the constant transition between these opposites that creates the enormous power typical of the highly trained Chen Taiji boxer. While the science behind this power development is rooted in Chinese metaphysics, it is accessible to any practitioner. Maintaining a balance of forces produces a flexible power that permits the body to move with Chen Taiji's torquing quality at any speed and rhythm. And it is through form practice that this difficult-to-master skill is obtained.

To achieve the ability to twine or torque the body, you must understand the distinction between the forces of Yin and Yang. The side of the body that is weight-bearing is considered to be Yang, while the opposite side of the body, not subject to tension, is considered Yin. As the weight shifts from left to right or front to back, so do the forces of Yin and Yang in the body. Chen boxing emphasizes a clear, visible distinction of these forces. Thus, when you first practice the forms, it is not easy on the legs. Each side of the lower body must be conditioned to control the practitioner's weight, to launch powerful moves during physical transitions of technique.

The techniques are designed around the style's unique twining movement, infused with chan szu jin. Directed by the waist and powered by a rooted stance, focused twining movement is characteristic of Chen masters. Highly developed chan szu jin imbues Chen Taiji with the inimitable explosiveness unique to Chen boxers. In Chen Taijiquan, this power is highly refined and fuels the fighting techniques recorded in the forms.

Most important, control over these bodily forces must emanate from the area about two inches below the navel. Called the Dantian, this central point of the body is considered the storehouse of internal energy—known as "qi" or "chi." According to Chen boxing methodology, the boxer's "silk reeling" movement originates and ends with the Dantian. So when practicing, seek to originate all movement from the Dantian, and measure your ability to do so as an indication of progress.

Master Ren Guang Yi

One of the world's leading twelfth-generation Chen Taiji masters, Ren Guang Yi is the premier disciple of Grandmaster Chen Xiaowang. Master Ren dedicated ten years to full-time study under Grandmaster Chen in Chenjiagou village and in Zhengzhou, Henan, China. By undergoing highly rigorous training in the forms, fighting, and weapons training of traditional Chen style, Master Ren has distinguished himself as America's premier Chen Taiji master.

In 1991 Master Ren founded the ICSTA in New York, while pursuing an illustrious career in teaching and competitions. After winning grand championships in the United States, Master Ren took first place in the heavyweight division at the 1998 International Taijiquan Competition held in Wenxian, Henan, China. Master Ren has produced some of the finest Chen practitioners in the U.S. today. His senior students have emerged as leading competitors, teachers, and scholars of Chen Taiji. In addition to his teaching and competitive success, Master Ren's ICSTA-produced video series on Chen Taiji is highly regarded and extremely popular.

Currently, Master Ren travels globally, offering seminars on a wide variety of Chen Taiji subjects, while continuing his popular long-running classes in the New York tri-state area. To learn more about Master Ren and Chen Taiji, please visit the ICSTA Web site at http://www.chentaijiquan.com.

Stephan Berwick and **Jose Figueroa** were among Master Ren's small group of original students. Both came to Chen style Taijiquan after devoting many years to other martial arts. Currently they remain active practitioners, devoted to the mastery and promotion of Chen Taiji.

Mr. Berwick's thirty years of Chinese martial arts experience span China, Hong Kong, and the United States. Under the auspices of Master Bow Sim Mark of the Chinese Wushu Research Institute, Mr. Berwick was one of only two Americans (along with Hong Kong film star Donnie Yen, son of Bow Sim Mark) certified as martial arts instructors at the Xi'an Athletic Technical Institute in Shaanxi, China. While in China, Mr. Berwick was personally trained by China's national champion, Zhao Chang Jun and national-level coach Bai Wenxiang. Mr. Berwick went on to be a professional martial artist for many years, spending two of those years in Hong Kong as an action performer for Hong Kong film director Yuen Wo Ping, working alongside Donnie Yen. In August 2000 Master Ren brought Mr. Berwick to China to conduct primary research on Chen Taiji's twelfth-generation family members, Chen style training techniques, and Chen Taiji history at Chenjiagou village.

Grand Master Chen Xiaowang (seated) and Master Ren Guang Yi with senior disciples (left to right) Stephan J. Berwick, Jose M. Figueroa, and Greg Pinney

Mr. Berwick holds a B.A. in Literature and an M.A. in Law and Diplomacy, and currently works as a corporate manager, while writing on and teaching Chen Taijiquan. Since 1997 he has published numerous essays on Chen Taiji, one of which was chosen for the Advanced Training section of the 1999 Contemporary Books' *Ultimate Guide to Tai Chi*.

Jose Figueroa's seventeen years in Chinese martial arts include unrivaled success as one of America's premier internal Chinese martial arts competitors. He has won numerous grand championships and first place titles at every major Chinese martial arts tournament in the United States. As a national champion, he traveled to China with Master Ren in 1998 to train in Chen village and compete in the International Taiji Competition held in Wenxian, Henan, China.

With a B.S. in Physical Education, Mr. Figueroa has designed innovative physical education curricula based solely on Chinese martial arts, for the aged, at-risk youth, and the handicapped. He was the first to design and teach a physical education course composed of Chen Taiji and other Chinese martial arts for the New York City Board of Education. He also taught popular Taiji programs at the Wave Hill community, and the Equinox Health Club in New York City.

Since 1997, Mr. Figueroa emerged as one of New York's favorite theater choreographers. For his pioneering work with jazz composer and playwright, Fred Ho, Mr. Figueroa earned the 2000 NY Foundation for the Arts Gregory Millard fellowship for choreography, based on his use of Chinese martial arts for theater choreography. Also during this period, Mr. Figueroa served as an entertainment correspondent for *Kung Fu/Qigong* magazine.

Glossary

Canons of Boxing: A highly influential Chinese martial arts encyclopedia written by General Qi Jiquang, a prolific general from the sixteenth century.

Chan szu jing: The movement and path of internal energy, expressed in a coiling nature of the body.

Chenjiagou: The original Chen family village in Wenxian County, Henan Province, Northeast China.

Dantian: The storage depot of qi that is located about two inches beneath the navel.

Fa jing: The explosive issuing of relaxed power with any part of the body and imbued with the coiling characteristic of chan szu jing.

Lao Jia: The Chen Taijiquan Old Frame style, which is attributed to Chen Changxing.

Ming Dynasty: The last of the Han-dominated dynasties of China that survived into the seventeenth century.

Qi: The internal energy that circulates around specific pathways in the body, identified in Chinese medicine as meridians.

Xin Jia: The Chen Taijiquan New Frame style, which is attributed to Chen Fake.

Yi: Focused intention.

Yin & yang: The traditional Chinese philosophical concepts of opposites that conceptually define and seek balance in all endeavors.

BIBLIOGRAPHY

Berwick, Stephan. "Chen Taijiquan Combat Training." *Ultimate Guide to Tai Chi*, eds., John R. Little and Curtis F. Wong. Lincolnwood, IL: Contemporary Books, 1999. (Originally published in *Inside Kung Fu*, October 1997).

Chen, Xin. "Illustrated Explanations of Chen Family Boxing" (1929), translated from the Chinese by Jarek Szymanski. Jarek's Chinese Martial Arts Page, 1999. http://www.chinafrominside.com/ma/taiji/chenxin.html.

Gu, Liuxin, Zhiqiang Feng, Dabiao Feng, Xiaowang Chen. *Chen Style Taijiquan*. Hong Kong: Hai Feng and Zhaohua, 1984.